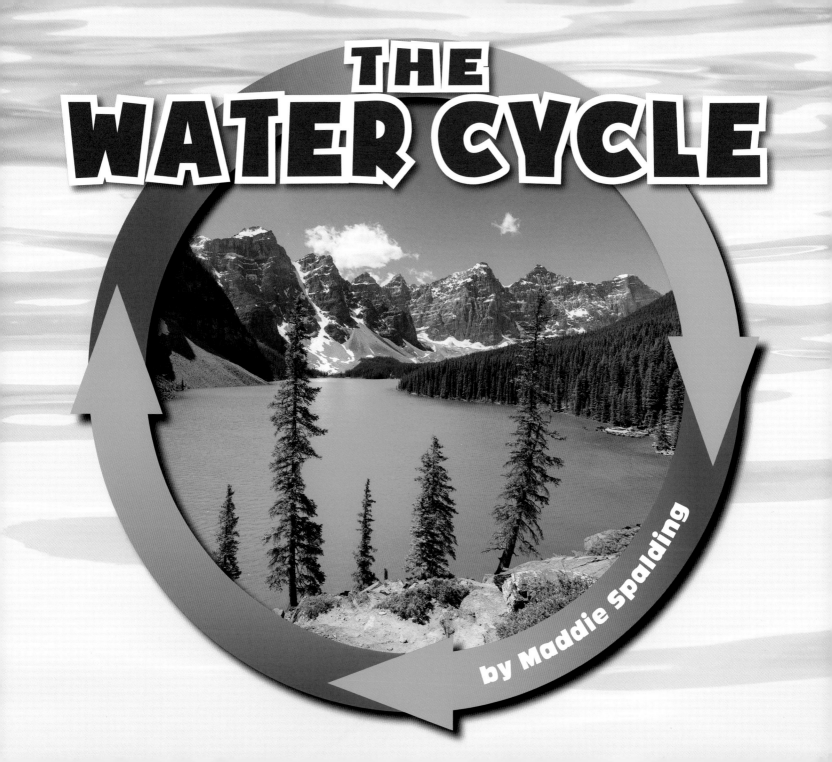

THE WATER CYCLE

by Maddie Spalding

The Child's World®
childsworld.com

Published by The Child's World®
1980 Lookout Drive • Mankato, MN 56003-1705
800-599-READ • www.childsworld.com

ISBN 9781503828513
LCCN 2018944809

Printed in the United States of America
PAO2396

About the Author

Maddie Spalding is a writer and editor
who lives in Minneapolis, Minnesota.
She has written more than 20 books
for children.

Table of Contents

CHAPTER ONE
Water Everywhere

Water is everywhere. It is above your head on a cloudy day. It drops from clouds as rain. It forms lakes and rivers. It turns into ice and snow.

Water is always moving around Earth. This movement is called the water cycle. Because of this cycle, water can take on different forms. Water can exist as a liquid, gas, or solid.

Water is made up of **molecules**. A molecule is the smallest unit of a substance that still has all the qualities of the substance. Water molecules are always moving. Molecules in a liquid flow freely. Water in liquid form makes up lakes and other bodies of water. Rain is also liquid water.

Animals need water to survive.

Molecules move quickly when water is heated. They start to spread out and take up more space. Then the water turns into a gas. Water usually becomes a gas when it reaches 212 degrees Fahrenheit (100°C). Water in gas form is called water vapor.

A liquid that is cooled can become a solid. Water freezes at 32 degrees Fahrenheit (0°C) and becomes a solid. Snow and ice are solid forms of water. Molecules in a solid are close together.

Snow is one important part of the water cycle.

Water is important in all of its forms. Water vapor moves through the **atmosphere**. It forms clouds. Rain comes from clouds. Rain helps plants grow. It also fills up lakes and other bodies of water. Many plants and animals live in these bodies of water. People get water from man-made lakes called reservoirs. Rain helps fill up reservoirs. Water also falls from clouds as snow. Snow helps control the temperature of Earth's surface. Snow that melts can help fill up reservoirs.

The water cycle is constant. Water has been flowing on Earth for billions of years. The water cycle distributes water all around the world. All of this water supports life on Earth. People, plants, and animals rely on this water every day.

People use reservoirs as a water supply source.

CHAPTER TWO

From Cloud to Raindrop

Most of Earth's surface is covered in water. Oceans make up much of this water. Other bodies of water include lakes and rivers. Sunlight heats the water's surface. This surface water then changes form. It becomes a gas. This process is called evaporation.

Sunlight also heats soil and plants. Soil and plants contain water. They release water vapor as temperatures increase. This process is called transpiration.

Water vapor is lighter than air. It rises into the atmosphere. Water vapor is a **greenhouse gas**. Greenhouse gases surround Earth. Sunlight warms Earth's surface. Earth's surface cools at night and releases some heat back into the atmosphere. Water vapor absorbs some of this heat. This helps trap heat in Earth's atmosphere. Life would not exist on Earth if temperatures were too cold. Water vapor helps keep Earth warm.

People can see the process of evaporation over very hot water.

Water vapor cools as it rises. This is because air high up in the atmosphere is cooler than air near Earth's surface. The vapor **condenses** as it cools. It changes from a gas to a liquid. It becomes water droplets. These small drops of water pick up **particles** in the air. The particles may include salt or dust. The droplets form clouds. Droplets collide inside a cloud. Then they form larger droplets. Large droplets can become heavy enough that they fall from the cloud. It takes millions of water droplets to form a raindrop.

When water vapor inside clouds begins forming raindrops, clouds will change to a dark color.

Ice crystals may also form inside a cloud. This happens when the temperature around the cloud is at or below 32 degrees Fahrenheit (0°C). The crystals stick together. Then they become heavy enough to fall to the ground. They fall as snow or ice. The temperature in the low atmosphere below the clouds may be above 32 degrees Fahrenheit (0°C). Then the snow will melt and falls as rain. The snow won't melt if temperatures are below 32 degrees Fahrenheit (0°C). It will fall to the ground as snow. It may also fall as hail or sleet. Sleet is frozen rain. These are all forms of **precipitation**. Some of this water flows into bodies of water. Then the water cycle begins all over again.

Hail falls most often in the summer.

CHAPTER THREE

Climate Change

The water cycle is continuous. It occurs naturally. But changes in **climate** can affect the water cycle. Climate change is a change in global weather patterns. These patterns include the average amount of rainfall in an area.

Many scientists believe climate change can be caused by pollution. Pollution occurs when people burn **fossil fuels**. Fossil fuels are a type of energy source. Coal and natural gas are common fossil fuels. People use these fuels to power machines and produce electricity. Burning fossil fuels releases **pollutants** into the atmosphere.

Trash pollution can harm the environment.

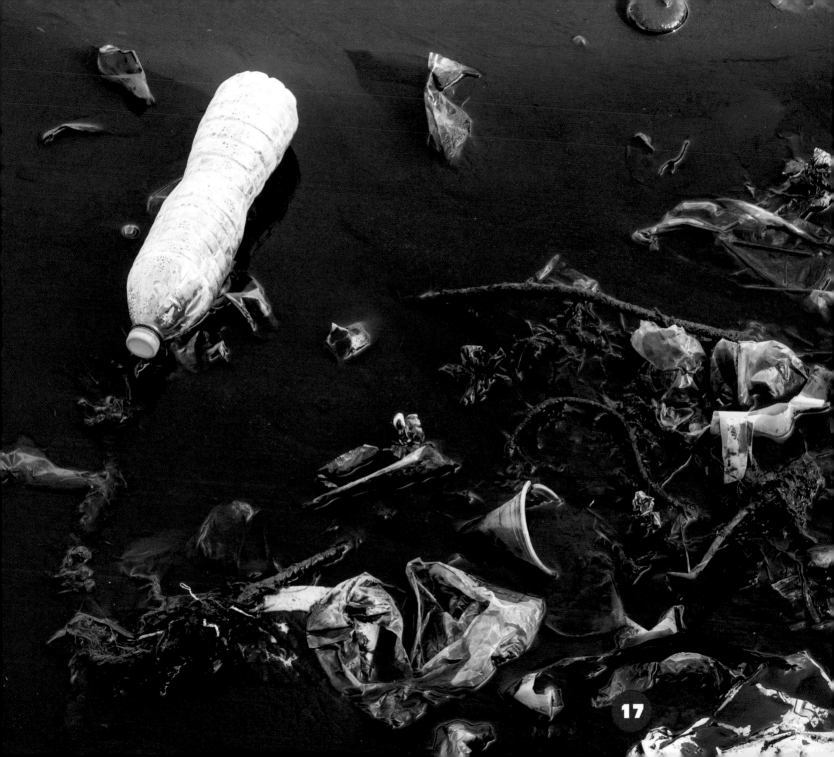

Deforestation

Deforestation can also affect the water cycle. Deforestation is the removal of many trees in an area. Trees may be cut down for many reasons. Wood can be used as fuel. Trees may be removed to make space for buildings or farms. Trees play a part in the water cycle. They release water vapor. When trees are cut down, less water vapor enters the atmosphere. Then the climate in an area may change. Less rain may fall. This can cause droughts.

These pollutants include carbon dioxide. Carbon dioxide is a greenhouse gas. It occurs naturally in Earth's atmosphere. But burning fossil fuels increases the amount of carbon dioxide in the atmosphere. More heat is trapped in the atmosphere as the amount of greenhouse gases increase. Temperatures rise at Earth's surface. More water evaporates as temperatures increase. Then clouds are more likely to form. This can result in intense rainstorms. These rainstorms can cause flooding.

A rise in temperatures also dries out soil. Dry soil and increased temperatures can cause drought. Drought occurs when an area receives little or no rain for a long period of time.

Climate change may disrupt the water cycle. But people are making changes to fight climate change. Some people are using different fuels instead of fossil fuels. People around the world recognize the importance of the water cycle. Making these changes may help protect it.

Some companies cut down trees to make paper and wood products.

The Water Cycle

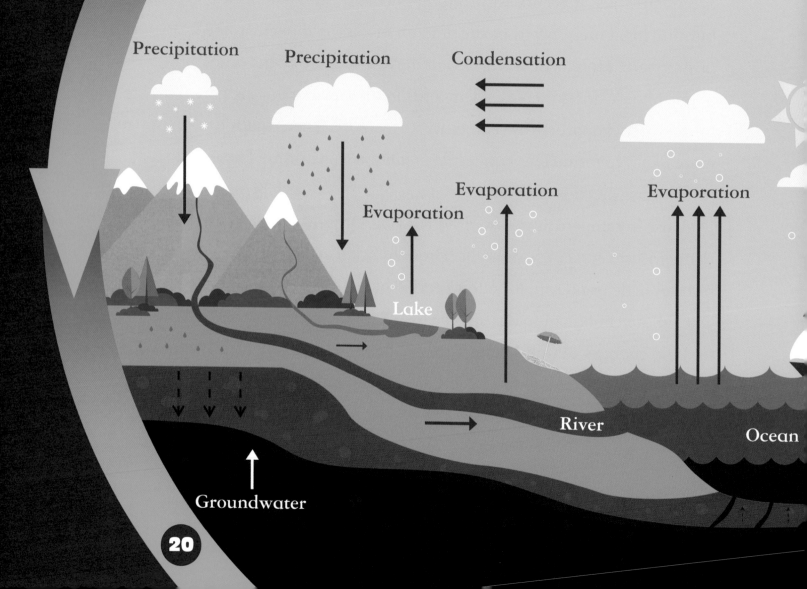

Precipitation

Precipitation

Condensation

Evaporation

Evaporation

Evaporation

Lake

River

Ocean

Groundwater

Fast Facts

- Water is constantly changing its form as it moves through Earth's atmosphere. This continuous movement of water is called the water cycle.

- Water turns from a liquid to a gas during evaporation. Sunlight heats the surface of lakes, oceans, and other bodies of water. Water at the surface turns into a gas. Water as a gas is called water vapor.

- Water vapor cools as it rises in Earth's atmosphere. It turns from a gas to a liquid. Water vapor becomes water droplets. This process is called condensation.

- Water droplets in a cloud collide with each other and stick together. When a water drop becomes heavy enough, it falls from the cloud. The water drop can become rain, snow, or other forms of precipitation.

- Climate change can affect the water cycle. It can cause flooding or drought.

Glossary

atmosphere (AT-muhs-feer) The atmosphere is the gases surrounding Earth. Water vapor moves through Earth's atmosphere.

climate (KLYE-mit) Climate is the usual weather conditions in an area over a period of time. Climate can affect the water cycle.

condenses (kuhn-DENS-iz) When something condenses, it turns from a gas into a liquid. Water vapor condenses into water droplets as it cools.

fossil fuels (FAH-suhl FYOO-uhlz) Fossil fuels are organic materials formed from dead organisms that may be burned. Natural gas and coal are fossil fuels.

greenhouse gas (GREEN-howss GASS) A greenhouse gas is a gas that traps heat in Earth's atmosphere. Water vapor is a greenhouse gas.

molecules (MAH-luh-kyoolz) Molecules are groups of atoms that join together and have special properties. Water has molecules.

particles (PAR-ti-kuhlz) Particles are small pieces or amounts of something. Water droplets pick up particles.

pollutants (puh-LOO-tuhnts) Pollutants are substances that pollute or contaminate the environment. Burning fossil fuels releases pollutants such as carbon dioxide.

precipitation (pri-sip-i-TAY-shun) Precipitation is water in any form that falls to the ground. Rain, snow, hail, and sleet are forms of precipitation.

To Learn More

IN THE LIBRARY

Dickmann, Nancy. *The Water Cycle*.
New York, NY: Cavendish Square, 2016.

Linde, Barbara M. *The Water Cycle*.
New York, NY: Gareth Stevens Publishing, 2017.

Miller, Mirella S. *Life in Freshwater Lakes*.
Mankato, MN: The Child's World, 2015.

ON THE WEB

Visit our Web site for links about the water cycle:
childsworld.com/links

Note to Parents, Teachers, and Librarians: We routinely verify our Web links to make sure they are safe and active sites. So encourage your readers to check them out!

Index